FINISHING LINE PRESS

www.finishinglinepress.com

Translate Sun/Son/Sum

poems by

Lyz Soto

Finishing Line Press
Georgetown, Kentucky

Translate Sun/Son/Sum

ACKNOWLEDGMENTS

The equation included in "All Descended From…" and "Sun:" is the Hardy-
Weinberg Principle, which is a genetic theorem concerning the consistency of
genotype and allele frequencies in populations.

"Pacific Coordinates" was previously published in the journal, *Hawai'i Review
Issue 79: Call and Response*.

Publisher: Leah Maines

Editor: Christen Kincaid

Cover Art: Joy Enomoto

Author Photo: Jakob Bauwens

Cover Design: Elizabeth Maines McCleavy

Printed in the USA on acid-free paper.
Order online: www.finishinglinepress.com
              also available on amazon.com

Author inquiries and mail orders:
Finishing Line Press
P. O. Box 1626
Georgetown, Kentucky 40324
U. S. A.

Table of Contents

for Jakob

darkening limbs darkening limbs darkening limbs darkening limbs darkening limbs
darkening limbs darkening limbs darkening limbs darkening limbs darkening limbs
darkening limbs darkening limbs darkening limbs darkening limbs darkening limbs
darkening limbs darkening limbs darkening limbs darkening limbs darkening limbs
darkening limbs darkening limbs darkening limbs darkening limbs darkening limbs
darkening limbs darkening limbs darkening limbs darkening limbs darkening limbs
darkening limbs darkening limbs darkening limbs darkening limbs darkening limbs
darkening limbs darkening limbs darkening limbs darkening limbs darkening limbs
darkening limbs darkening limbs darkening limbs darkening limbs darkening limbs
darkening limbs darkening limbs darkening limbs darkening limbs darkening limbs
darkening limbs darkening limbs darkening limbs darkening limbs darkening limbs
darkening limbs darkening limbs darkening limbs darkening limbs darkening limbs
darkening limbs darkening limbs darkening limbs darkening limbs darkening limbs
darkening limbs darkening limbs darkening limbs darkening limbs darkening limbs
darkening limbs darkening limbs darkening limbs darkening limbs darkening limbs
darkening limbs darkening limbs darkening limbs darkening limbs darkening limbs
darkening limbs darkening limbs darkening limbs darkening limbs darkening limbs
darkening limbs darkening limbs darkening limbs darkening limbs darkening limbs
darkening limbs darkening limbs darkening limbs darkening limbs darkening limbs
darkening limbs darkening limbs darkening limbs darkening limbs darkening limbs
darkening limbs darkening limbs darkening limbs darkening limbs darkening limbs
darkening limbs darkening limbs darkening limbs darkening limbs darkening limbs
darkening limbs darkening limbs darkening limbs darkening limbs darkening limbs
darkening limbs darkening limbs darkening limbs darkening limbs darkening limbs
darkening limbs darkening limbs darkening limbs darkening limbs darkening limbs
darkening limbs darkening limbs darkening limbs darkening limbs darkening limbs
darkening limbs darkening limbs darkening limbs darkening limbs darkening limbs
darkening limbs darkening limbs darkening limbs darkening limbs darkening limbs
darkening limbs darkening limbs darkening limbs darkening limbs darkening limbs
darkening limbs darkening limbs darkening limbs darkening limbs darkening limbs
darkening limbs darkening limbs darkening limbs darkening limbs darkening limbs
darkening limbs darkening limbs darkening limbs darkening limbs darkening limbs
darkening limbs darkening limbs darkening limbs darkening limbs darkening limbs
darkening limbs darkening limbs darkening limbs darkening limbs darkening limbs
darkening limbs darkening limbs darkening limbs darkening limbs darkening limbs
darkening limbs darkening limbs darkening limbs darkening limbs darkening limbs
darkening limbs darkening limbs darkening limbs darkening limbs darkening limbs
darkening limbs darkening limbs darkening limbs darkening limbs darkening limbs
darkening limbs darkening limbs darkening limbs darkening limbs darkening limbs
darkening limbs darkening limbs darkening limbs darkening limbs darkening limbs

In the Bodleian

It started cobbled, but
reduced to sensible mortar.

Blue lips against
glass stained kissing the outside
frost holding warm light
stacked and rolled
in vellum in tissue

coveted from the separate state.
Barred by habit, but
worshiped. When did word
turn wanton turn licentious. Get
a Beatrix cottage sideshow. Just
a sneak of rosemary and thyme
of this repository
in a flattering perspective.
Remember their gaze
their hands on all our stones.
Nothing hocked
nor thieved nor plundered. Please.

Wrapped in quest
I give my latchkeys.
I offer passwords
and incantations.
Alpha. Numeric. Symbols.
Anything for a minute peep.

All Descended from…

We must begin with:

$$f_1(A) - f_1(AA) + \frac{1}{2} f_1(Aa) = p^2 + pq(p+q) = p = f_0(A)$$

to translate:

In this land
   without winter,
do we coddle the sun
    or leave her,

         trust

 she will behave,

         ignore

her folded body
around his folded body
nestled water folding
around their folding
bodies?

Do we leave her pitched
high and bursting?

        Nowhere to land
        no one to stand
        no one to say

yes, rest here
when you are tired

        black, arms
        half circled open, welcome.

Translation II

In hardwood quiet
Might I chase my letters,
herd them to words,
or shoo them to
hidden corners/rest
in nothing/relief
there is no one calling
my name.
Will I stop or
ask or trust
he is okay
in the next quiet?

Will I say nothing
about how he
cleaned his room,   when I didn't ask.

Give nothing
when he holds his hand out/open/asks for praise.
Hesitate
if he asks
for a hug.   I am busy.

Will I leave him waiting hoping for   *one*   *hint*   *yes.*
I love him.
Yes
in italics, in capitals
and even
in lower case
letters.

Dois Café, Duas Cores Redução and Other Bifurcated Fallacies

Stammered walk into the closest corner café, one
in a long stroke of many. We were hungry for Lisboa.
We sat. Almost asked for eggs masquerading as tortillas, when
He said in supple rolling r's. He said in our still blank faces.
Repeated and repeated

when another He, in quiet brown skin, He said
you can eat in that café over there if you want. He said
they'll serve you there if you want. He said
to our blank faces, when someone Brown said
Blacks eat here.

They serve Whites there.
Americano? They'll be okay with you there.
Our blank faces stilled, when someone, one of We said can
We eat here?

Do We Coddle the Sun

Definition: Sun: a star at the center of our solar system. It is approximately 99% of our solar system's mass. It is a G2V yellow star. Comprised mostly of hydrogen, but also contains helium, oxygen, carbon, iron, neon, nitrogen, silicon, magnesium, and sulfur. In the edge of the corona, filaments of plasma stretch across the surface, dancing. Considered as an idealized black body with darkening limbs, as the center appears brighter than the outer rim. The Sun spirals the Milky Way on Orion's Arm more than 25,000 light years from this galaxy's heart. It is roughly 4 and a half billion years old, formed in a cloud of molecular gases, it will grow ever hotter until it cools to a white dwarf bright and dying.

> We spin to the lyre
> of the dead Luna almanac
> dazzled by days of Sol.

Sun

Homonym: Son:

Don't you think son right after you hear sun, or do you think moon.

son/mother/parent/person/son/mother/parent/person   son/mother/parent/person/
son/mother/parent/person/   son/mother/parent/person/   son/mother/parent/person/
son/mother/parent/person/   son/mother/parent/person/   son/mother/parent/person/
son/mother/parent/person/   son/mother/parent/person/   son/mother/parent/person/
son/mother/parent/person/ son/mother/parent/person/ son/mother/parent/person/ person/
son/mother/ son/mother/parent/person/ son/mother/parent/person/ son/mother/parent/person/
son/mother/parent/person/   son/mother/parent/person/   son/mother/parent/person/
son/mother/parent/person/   son/mother/parent/person/   son/mother/parent/person/
son/mother/parent/person/   son/mother/parent/person/   son/mother/parent/person/
son/mother/parent/person/   mother/parent/person/   son/mother/parent/person/
son/mother/parent/person/ son/mother/parent/person/ son/mother/parent/person/ person/
son/mother/son/   mother/parent/person/   son/mother/parent/person/
son/mother/parent/person/   son/mother/parent/person/   son/mother/parent/person/
son/mother/parent/person// son/mother/parent/person/ son/ son/mother/parent/person/
son/mother/parent/person/ son/mother/parent/   person/ son/mother/parent/person/
son/mother/parent/person/ son/mother/parent/person/   son son/mother/parent/person/
son/mother/parent/person/ son/mother/parent/person/ son/ mother/parent/person/
son/mother/parent/person/ son/mother/parent/person/ son/ mother/parent/ person/
son/mother/parent/person/   son/mother/parent/person/ son/mother/parent/person/
son/mother/parent/person/   /mother/parent/person/son/mother/parent/person/
son/mother/parent/person/ son/mother/parent/person/ son/ mother/parent/person/
son/mother/parent/person/   son/mother/parent/person/   son/mother/parent/person/
son/mother/parent/person/   son/mother/parent/person/   son/mother/parent/person/
son/mother/parent/person/   son/mother/parent/person/   son/mother/parent/person/
son/mother/parent/person/   son/mother/parent/person/   son/mother/parent/person/
son/mother/parent/person/   son/mother/parent/person/   son/mother/parent/person/
son/mother/parent/person/   son/mother/parent/person/   son/mother/parent/person/
son/mother/parent/person/   son/mother/parent/person/   son/mother/parent/person/
son/mother/parent/person/   son/mother/parent/person/   son/mother/parent/person/
son/mother/parent/person/   son/mother/parent/person/   son/mother/parent/person/
son/mother/parent/person/

which comes first.

Tropical

They loved the Hawai'i thing, like exotic like cool
like where's your grass skirt, like how come   *Joke.*
you dress like us....like serious it's thirty degrees   *Serious.*
outside! How do you think I should dress! My coconut bra
isn't insulated.

But they didn't trust my expert body, like I was suspect
like I was fallible, because Americans can't read
maps. He said, I'm positive Hawaii is in the Caribbean,
and I said, I'm pretty positive   *And I shouldn't have*
it's not. He hunted that word through my sentence. He isolated *said pretty, which*
and culled it on his tongue, then presented back to me   *sounded unsure,*
on pink buds, an ignorant gift of my home. He said   *which could have
been a disclaimer,*
if I'm right you'll drink the full glass. I said   *which might have*
if I'm right you'll feel like an idiot. And   *meant I*
I never drank the full glass, but even mistaken oceans and   *didn't believe my*
thousands of misplaced miles   *own expert body.*
didn't stop him from asking over and over
about sandwiches and cold meat. Talking about how
he wanted to take at least one
bite.

But they asked how I stayed tan in the dead
grey of winter. They wondered if I snuck home
to sub-tropical skies, when no one was looking.
How could I still be almost
brown? and funny how no one ever thought this
was my born color so almost different
so almost the same.

But I was struck hard
by their northern bodies spaced out on grass pieces   *My mother thought they*
whenever the sun threatened to show face. They   *looked like dead bodies*
were so white their veins pulsed   *littering the park.*
blue as throbbing cobalt sub dermal branches lit

beneath a drumming yellow star.

And I was struck by their abandonment
to the heady warmth of fifty degrees,   *Fahrenheit, not Celsius.*
so seductive with their exotic speech
their adamant horizontal postures impenetrable by arctic flutter.
I saw them as tough even in their crisp fragile
whites and I know
at least one of them
saw me
as an edible
bite too spicy to take home to a respectable acceptable
three bedroom semi in quiet Devon.

Translation VII

I   make   her
                  Hiʻiaka breasted, hipped
                            and blaring.
                    I call her

                Fahrenheit, not Celsius.
she not he

           convinced for five millennia
                  fathers have been
                        wrong.

Men made her
male: opposite of emasculate:
antonym of this: to empower with testicles.

They   sheared   her curves

                      cast her as
                          a battle cry and killing

           never warming never
           stifled never

waiting home
for children.

become a new branch become a new branch become a new branch become a new
branch become a new branch become a new branch become a new branch become
a new branch become a new branch become a new branch become a new branch
become a new branch become a new branch become a new branch become a new
branch become a new branch become a new branch become a new branch become
a new branch become a new branch become a new branch become a new branch
become a new branch become a new branch become a new branch become a new
branch become a new branch become a new branch become a new branch become
a new branch become a new branch become a new branch become a new branch
become a new branch become a new branch become a new branch become a new
branch become a new branch become a new branch become a new branch become
a new branch become a new branch become a new branch become a new branch
become a new branch become a new branch become a new branch become a new
branch become a new branch become a new branch become a new branch become
a new branch become a new branch become a new branch become a new branch
become a new branch become a new branch become a new branch become a new
branch become a new branch become a new branch become a new branch become
a new branch become a new branch become a new branch become a new branch
become a new branch become a new branch become a new branch become a new
branch become a new branch become a new branch become a new branch become
a new branch become a new branch become a new branch become a new branch
become a new branch become a new branch become a new branch become a new
branch become a new branch become a new branch become a new branch become
a new branch become a new branch become a new branch become a new branch
become a new branch become a new branch become a new branch become a new
branch become a new branch become a new branch become a new branch become
a new branch become a new branch become a new branch become a new branch
become a new branch become a new branch become a new branch become a new
branch become a new branch become a new branch become a new branch become
a new branch become a new branch become a new branch become a new branch
become a new branch become a new branch become a new branch become a new
branch become a new branch become a new branch become a new branch become
a new branch become a new branch become a new branch become a new branch
become a new branch become a new branch become a new branch become a new
branch become a new branch become a new branch become a new branch become
a new branch become a new branch become a new branch become a new branch
become a new branch become a new branch become a new branch become a new
branch become a new branch become a new branch become a new branch become a
new branch become a new branch become a new branch become a new branch become
a new branch become a new branch become a new branch become a new branch
becomeanewbranchbecomeanewbranchbecomeanewbranchbecomeanewbranch

Staging Hybrid Hygiene

Miss Saigon meets
surrealism
at west
ends and Eurasian
is villain is yellow
faced with a beautiful
voice and no
name looking creepy
from sitting half
a mile away spying
him displaying
prosthetics for eyes
and flesh. Just
theater pretend, right?
Just jokes, right?
No serious
in this royal
box,
instead debate
erupts in blaring
broad paved lights.
Save money on face
paint!! Hire
Asian actors for
Asian roles! But
where to begin
with Asian passing
for Eurasian
Amerasian hello bloody
mixed this body
into halves then
quarts then eighths
then sixteenths then
who acts us
to reduction? Simmer

down to performing
an eclectic skin.
Under a micro lens
look at Baigaur
or Prey Nokor
become Sài Gòn
become Gia
Định become Saïgon
become a Thành phố Hồ Chí
Minh villain and see
his loose
quilted stitches.
Watch
the careless sewn
not quite hold
him together.

Translation X

Habilis, erectus, neanderthalensis
before *sapiens*, did they
see pantheons in night skies. Did they picture
the sun a devastating god. Did they see she
as he. Did they see him as swallowing
worlds. Did they burn sand
into glass, dissect the universe
into strings, and try to become singular
beings. They did not see the sun
as middle ground average. Can the star
imagine himself as modest when they would
make him hierophant and order; when they
would look up in the sky; find the reason
for everything and become a new branch.

Sun:

$$f_1(A) - f_1(AA) + \frac{1}{2} f_1(Aa) = p^2 + pq(p+q) = p = f_0(A)$$

Sum is not
a homonym of sun.
but rhymes with my son
greater than all my parts
beloved
number cells
divided
multiplied to a son
with his own sum,
equated.
molecular markers give him
19p13.1-q13.11
not seen by me
not predicted blond
fair skin
black eyes, but
this is how 3,000,000,000
=1>2, where he started
in 2, who didn't see 1
as possible.

Asylum: Empire Settlement Act Revisited Re-enacted Reincarnated

Not older than ten years
little African girl lay
her over large clothes spread winged
across that vented
metal web embedded sidewalk
exhaling heat into
late December midnight. She slept
in uninhibited precarious childhood.
As we watched.
As Millais in his fortunate slim suit bent
to his glossy heels
tucked a paper bill
into a thinned shirt pocket
as little girl slept her unconscious asylum.

Translation XI

give her asylum
make this space fetal
as she describes almost insignificant
percentages to guesses there
are no tests to assess risk but
trace this gambit in twists
and ladder shoots and shifts
a gap in ropes and molecular
strings predicting her baby's
grey matter waves safe
and stable not chemical branched
unbalanced or environmental
triggered she would risk
that toss again in Markov
chains she does not flinch
from probability processes
just let her guess yes he
will probably smile again
even after he's been
pinkie promised with grief sitting
in the same seat as his believing
tomorrow it has to get better
again

$$H = 1.7 \times 10^8 a^{-1/10} M_{16}^{-3/20} \, m_1^{-3/8} R_{10}^{9/8} f^{3/5} \text{cm}$$

$$T = 1.4 \times 10^4 a^{-1/5} M_{16}^{3/10} m_1^{1/4} R_{10}^{-3/4} f^{6/5} K$$

$$p = 3.1 \times 10^{-8} a^{-7/10} M_{16}^{11/20} m_1^{5/8} R_{10}^{-15/8} f^{11/5} \text{g cm}^{-3}$$

Imposing Desires

I bought the old world legend.
Darwin was sexy
especially when he
got social with Galton
said only the vigorous
should survive.

Don't you think
tropical tastes
better supped
with eugenics wearing
flossy petticoats
and woolen
skirts? I wanted
to go there, where they
thought image
was akin to salvation.
And sweating
with fractured ribs
meant certain sainthood.

Please
Beretania me
because Chippendale
Wedgewood Kipling
Shelley and Mill
were varnished
with alluring gestures
and didn't domanial caresses
tempt imitation
like white linen Conrad
Cook Magna Carter
Bilbo Sherwood.

Amalgamate me

into Liverpool
London Skowhegan
New York Bennington
and Berlin this
singular exotic body looming
at eastern horizons.

Give me
a gilded bunny
clutched to my
breast gorged
on carrots
and cabbage
dressed in blue
velvet.

In my school
every lesson
book said
this direction held
the promised this way
towards the canon
home. Where I might beg
interpellation covered
me with icing
mix me as palatable
new world sweet
as sucking kō
midday
on a haul road
sitting toes digging
intosoft powdered dirt.

West

Perfect, she thought perfect of this
outstretched land invented gun
powder red paper flutter litter Baba
she cried what made them pretty?
Narcissus blooms. Baba, forgive my
flower. Wilted bud forever white
no crimson no blush my bleached
blood, she said. Baba, on trade
pacific winds hear me. Your
Daughter. Still. waiting.   over
        there.   where
you left me.

                                                  Blank:
                                   no portrait
                                   no text
                                       just
                                          contrails
                                   or wakes
                                   perhaps outlines
                            shades-ancestors-
                       chains-anchors-
                              cut

                  by Grandpa:
                      sepia-d grin to his gums
                      He said…,asked, Why
                      go back? Why?
              Tagalog/Ilokano/Visayan/Spanish
      and more named Austronesian/Malyao-
                        Polynesian
                 almost Hawai`i
              almost America
                              English.

              Almost Home waves
          washed white capped
     swells lapping volcanic sipping coral
sluicing reef. He spoke on my
    deaf ears. Now
               I guess
                He said, let them go, these
          words drop or toss them to swirling
          currents. Yes. He said, yes
       let them fall
         shallow and hollow
                                   drift.
                    They have
             no place
        here.

Intentions

In 1 billion years, our sun will burn too hot. This earth will boil waterless.
Will we still be fighting over land. Will our bodies forget about bleeding.
Forget primordial. Forget ooze. Will we regret the sea. We never returned.
Anchored our soles on parchment and stone. We feared its rise. Resented
its salt. Will we miss drowning. Will hydrogen become sacred. In 3 billion
years more, the body of the sun will grow to not quite bursting. She
will engulf us to Mars/maybe/Jupiter will survive as she cools her slow
embrace.

> Then we will see
> at last the floor
> of the sea not hidden.

publife

you're american?

american: a proper noun microsoft insists on capital
for america for microsoft for philippines but not for welsh
for apache for kanaka maoli

yes.

you must be
apache or
navajo.

{oed says: welsh *v. a. n.* to swindle out
of money laid as a bet or to fail to keep
ones promise (obscure origin) or of
persons originally belonging to the
native british population of england}

no.

no? surely, you must be.

no i've enough cherokee
to fill a half pint but
that's not why
i look like this.

cherokee?
well, that explains
it, but i really
would have guessed
apache.

{oed says: apache is a people of athapascan Indians
(not from india) a member of this people, also
their language or a ruffian of a type infesting paris
also a man of ruffianly behavior}

i have no response to him,
native english vs. me, alien
sipping a half pint of bitter
with this thought cradled
in sudden american hands:
i don't even know what
apache
is.

microsoft finds no capital in kanaka.

{oed says: kanaka is a native of the south sea
islands, especially one employed in
queensland as a labourer on the sugar
plantations, (obscure) also the hawaiian

find a half pint of cherokee.

{oed says: blood is the red liquid that
circulates in the arteries and veins of
man and the higher animals or also flesh
and blood: the distinctive characteristics
of the animal body hence equals
humanity as opposed to deity or other
disembodied spirit}

microsoft finds no word in maoli in kanaka maoli.

{oed says: maoli has no results}

{oed says: kanaka maoli has no results}

fill me from fingers to elbow with other.

{oed says: quantum is something
that has quantity}

Pax was Here Once

Beneath rivulets
        tattered mountains
                unearth, discover small
                        love Spoon with crags
                                and tides Swallow her
                                fire hair stroke his
                                        crooked hip. Gorge me
                                                with basalt-ed roots
                                                with feather trees
                                                with tendril-ed water
                                                in this found place
                                                this unintended
                                                                            home

New Echota
You   TAGGED   *we were here*
                         1838   on borrowed earth
but she almost erased you, shoved you in shoe boxes. I bet
you found it cramped. Musty in sinus skin. Sneezed and expelled
your own unwanted flesh. I hope   proud words described you, and
forgiveness lived without tight fists or chewed nails or bloodied lips. I must
believe   she loved you.   a half forgotten   imagined friend.   Convenient
when needed. When pretending safe was safe. and necessary.
On the inner side of my bottom lip not on Dawes Rolls   you
        TAGGED   *you were here*
                       1971
when there were still hills between Austin
and San Antonio. when Mom and Dad got still stares
for walking hand in beloved hand. when I still was a mixed language.
when I became the stutter the glottal stop the blot the blank slate. Stilled.

death happens

vitamins minerals calisthenics berries tea algae yoga run read
run pray run walk 30 minutes run read stop read prevention read
journals run read leaves eat ginger run tumeric drink lemon in 3
pray downward pray dog run 30 run 5 run 15 run private read
heart read stomach read colon love liver drink red chew ra
swallow sting swallow bite run sun run pray stop after stop
world make hades/abaddon/hina/enma-o gracious acquaintance
say

       look how crowded
       your house is no/no
       really i can't impose

                              Mihotoke ni idakarete
                                     Kimi yukinu nishi no kishi
                              Natsukashiki omokage mo
                                     Kiehateshi kanashisa yo
                              Mihotoke ni idakarete
                                     Kimi yukinu jihi no kuni
                              Misukui o mi ni kakete
                                     Shimeshimasu kashikosa yo
                              Mihotoke ni idakarete
                                     Kimi yukinu tama no ie
                              Utsukushiki mihotoke to
                                     Narimashishi tootosa yo

Translation XIV

Wouldn't it be great to
live forever. What
would that look like?

He said candy floss in the morning
brownies in the afternoon
potatoes, cheese, and sour cream at night
basketball and board games all day.

She wondered if he would
get tired from all that all the time. He
said Mommy, don't worry
we'd never get tired.

Today he said I think someday I'll
be ready to die. She asked him why
he stopped wanting to live forever? Maybe
someday, I'll get tired, he said, and
I know I don't want to be

forever
alone.

Cohabitation

Today
my skin
is fashionable
chic
designer
sometimes
drawn
quartered
wrapped and
parceled
in quantum
miscegeny
yet
cool
exotic
color
full, but
what if
tomorrow
militia or
cops come
armed
with jagged
teeth
with silver
bullets, hammering
fists big
lungs holler
today
you wash
the wrong
color
your DNA
blends
panic and

sweat but
I swear
yesterday
I
could
pass
pigments
against
paper bags, so
if tomorrow
other is
the wrong
color
will I
cry, yes find
my flesh
as cotton
with milk
like winter.

Stand Back

views shift at this distance
you have blurred
doctors say age as a question
corrective lenses frames
the picture on a crooked face
watch this hand twist
as hours pass with sleep
on the periphery
or am I Emma
Stone waking
up to dream Cameron
Crowe make me
blond blue eyed
and marriageable
and yes killing
answers the question

Bursting

Our sun won't supernova, so
no spectacular
for us.

no black hole future.

just a thermal pulse,
white dwarf,
slow cool,

winking to dim.

black out.

skin do I offer skin do I offer skin do I offer skin do I offer skin do I offer skin do
I offer skin do I offer skin do I offer skin do I offer skin do I offer skin do I offer
skin do I offer skin do I offer skin do I offer skin do I offer skin do I offer skin do
I offer skin do I offer skin do I offer skin do I offer skin do I offer skin do I offer
skin do I offer skin do I offer skin do I offer skin do I offer skin do I offer skin do
I offer skin do I offer skin do I offer skin do I offer skin do I offer skin do I offer
skin do I offer skin do I offer skin do I offer skin do I offer skin do I offer skin do
I offer skin do I offer skin do I offer skin do I offer skin do I offer skin do I offer
skin do I offer skin do I offer skin do I offer skin do I offer skin do I offer skin do I
offer skin do I offer skin do I offer skin do I offer skin do I offer skin do I offer skin
do I offer skin do I offer skin do I offer skin do I offer skin do I offer skin do I offer
skin do I offer skin do I offer skin do I offer skin do I offer skin do I offer skin do
I offer skin do I offer skin do I offer skin do I offer skin do I offer skin do I offer
skin do I offer skin do I offer skin do I offer skin do I offer skin do I offer skin do
I offer skin do I offer skin do I offer skin do I offer skin do I offer skin do I offer
skin do I offer skin do I offer skin do I offer skin do I offer skin do I offer skin do
I offer skin do I offer skin do I offer skin do I offer skin do I offer skin do I offer
skin do I offer skin do I offer skin do I offer skin do I offer skin do I offer skin do
I offer skin do I offer skin do I offer skin do I offer skin do I offer skin do I offer
skin do I offer skin do I offer skin do I offer skin do I offer skin do I offer skin do I
offer skin do I offer skin do I offer skin do I offer skin do I offer skin do I offer skin
do I offer skin do I offer skin do I offer skin do I offer skin do I offer skin do I offer
skin do I offer skin do I offer skin do I offer skin do I offer skin do I offer skin do
I offer skin do I offer skin do I offer skin do I offer skin do I offer skin do I offer
skin do I offer skin do I offer skin do I offer skin do I offer skin do I offer skin do I
offer skin do I offer skin do I offer skin do I offer skin do I offer skin do I offer skin
do I offer skin do I offer skin do I offer skin do I offer skin do I offer skin do I offer
skin do I offer skin do I offer skin do I offer skin do I offer skin do I offer skin do I
offer skin do I offer skin do I offer skin do I offer skin do I offer skin do I offer skin
do I offer skin do I offer skin do I offer skin do I offer skin do I offer skin do I offer
skin do I offer skin do I offer skin do I offer skin do I offer skin do I offer skin do
I offer skin do I offer skin do I offer skin do I offer skin do I offer skin do I offer
skin do I offer skin do I offer skin do I offer skin do I offer skin do I offer skin do I
offer skin do I offer skin do I offer skin do I offer skin do I offer skin do I offer skin
do I offer skin do I offer skin do I offer skin do I offer skin do I offer skin do I offer
skin do I offer skin do I offer skin do I offer skin do I offer skin do I offer skin do I
offer skin do I offer skin do I offer skin do I offer skin do I offer skin do I offer skin
do I offer skin do I offer skin do I offer skin do I offer skin do I offer skin do I offer
skin do I offer skin do I offer skin do I offer skin do I offer skin do I offer skin do
I offer skin do I offer skin do I offer skin do I offer skin do I offer skin do I offer
skin do I offer skin do I offer skin do I offer skin do I offer skin do I offer skin do
I offer skin do I offer skin do I offer skin do I offer skin do I offer skin do I offer

Reflections

Mercurial glass displays multi-faceted in mixed palettes. In
rainbows we convert to gradient which becomes
too ambiguous for the crowd. In downward slash they
diminish the composite to simple to one. Read their labels
all sharp angles in clear black lines cut through white bodies.
We gather reassurances through explicit concrete, basic
pigment black brown yellow red white blue purple blended
too muddied is too splattered so I become
canvases stretched thin and primed but accustom
to hydra reflections knowing they always see
what they fancy even in fun house glass.
Straddling Greenwich Meridian I wondered
if Su Xiao Xiao, Calamity Jane or Mary Magdalene
were the first to say I am anything you want me to be.

Taken for Granted

Have you ever

(because everything
is going so well)

looked the other way
not daring to think on could be
but

(because everything
is going too well)

an ambush
thought
sneaks in
dances with Arms flailing over head
a ridiculous ripped vicious grin
sings
please look at me you're
taking far
too much
for granted
      any minute now everything
      everything
will
go
wrong.

Translation XXI

In this foreign country, native tongues twist guileless.
Monsters stop on speechless. We always help strangers.
They have no blades, no full metal jackets, no shrapnel.
Predators   stay   gutless   figments....stained
pigments....but through these binoculars, look at them
crouched at his border. Slaver on their chins stalking
internet cafes, chat this room to a dungeon.

He would greet them with an upturned hand, bear wrist
welcome. My warnings sit pale ghosts on spikes. He
might see them, but heedless, he greets them with an
upturned hand, bear wrist welcome. Their disguise is
harmless. I interject. I object to flesh overtures.

But

I would not see him closed, Shut down, Haunted by
ghost head warnings, grotesque yawning gibbets, even
as they gibber over gluttonous feasts, even as they lick
the sprayed fat from their lips.

What skin do I offer?

Give him a hide:

Tell him pain is process, it blisters, a transitory tender
thin bubble, while new flesh roughens to callous to
another time to another time to another time makes skin
to harder to tear open.

RONGOPAI PAINTED

In smudges
in intricate scrolls, they charge   to bare
                 to charcoal
                 to scaped
                 to scraped red.
      They storm rage   by tackle
                              by strike
                              by shuffle
                              by muffled breath.
      They press eyes to cutout pockets,   through brushed panes
                              through battled grey
                              through brief light
                              through bent face.

Uncover your eyes
      unfold your shoulders
            open your fingers
                 see them   island hands
                              river throats
                              inlet cocks
                              mountain limbs
                              foothill breasts
                              ocean bellies
                              taproot wombs.

             Ear to stone, hear
                 listen to whakapapa from
                     line to line to line strung to tūpuna to
                          tūrangawaewae to Māoritanga.

                                    to waiata sing
                                        mana
                                        sing
                                          sky
                                        sing
                                        epa
                                        sing
                                flint water
                          lapping iron to grains

to salt metal sand shore.

Twist this thick alien tongue, speak
earth calling in lacquer in heart drops
from a graveled stomach through a cracked swallow
by a lanced eye I scry sink bowls and coriolis drains
searching for harbor.

First Impressions

I held no space for
a cobbled shore. Not in my head.
Not in my projected.

Nice I figured white
or yellow sand beaches automatic.
The cold clasped no surprise.

In Europe, in January,
warmth fled far south. We knew
even famed Riviera

cupped a chill. Long sleeves
stiff jeans flattened soled high tops
and down parkas were

our bathing suits. We
traveled far enough to demand
enjoyment, but fuck

if it wasn't cold.
Too frigid for cotton underwear
and tattered denim

acting as conduit
from refrigerated alluvion
soothed stones to butt

cheeks frozen to fatty
muscled blocks, I asked Why
would anyone ever

come here, even if it was
a hundred degrees outside…what?
…so you can burn

your ass on rocks
sunbathing? Impromptu traveling
companion one said

Says the bitch from Hawaii.
Impromptu traveling companion two, laid
out hooded and gloved said

I think she's right.
This is like glacial hell. Dani rubbed
eyes half circled

with shadows pressed deep
beneath the skin. She said
This is not what I imagined.

We sat. Watched crazed
worn men totter into the frosty sea.
Maybe Rome will be better.

Translation XXVIII

In this land of sun
there is no winter, no rest.
The sun longs for sleep.

Arms Half Circled

Impulse   sigh—   si—gn way— wa—ving   way— way—ward
       Black page   crippled   fear   all
   Scenarios   rocketonajetpack   BLAST

Stand

Shield

Protect

Edit

him

Stutter   mother

Stop

Stilt

Sour

him

Impulse   wave   wash   wander   neuron

I engrams

I pulse
to
pulse

I   am   pulse   in   cardiac flesh

I   ward   guard   gate
Stop
       Hand
             Stop
                 Sign
                     Stop   Him
                        stop.

thumbsucker

rustic. white wash.
affordable.
cheap pension. older. white. male. owner.
we were just leaving when
in gentle pulls he
sucked my thumb to its first knuckle
and i turned my face
to gag.

Open

I would dress
myself without
reserve, hang a
green light in my
window. But this
is not business
this sign swinging
on connective
sinew I can't read
backwards or
upside down
these letters are not
my flesh.

What skin am I
wearing if I see
you blood him if
I know if my son
salts one tear
bare handed still
still breathing I will
savage even your
bones to pieces.

thank you for this dance thank you for this dance

Intertalk

He wanted my straight hair
fingered while he palmed the flare
of ass cheek and under breast in
the whirling excuse of rhythm and notes.
He curled me to the floor and equilibrium
spun as optional. Through Tina's
mouth he said
in my home no one has your hair.
Through Tina's mouth
I did not answer. Just let the ground
brace me for the next spin, while
he spoke alphabets that Tina closed her lips over
tight and refused to spit with a small head shake
so I unraveled, untangled our skins in a twist and said
Thank you for this dance.

Translation XXXV

The engulfing sun reminds me of solar system has me thinking in roman
translates me to greek, I
am apollo/helios/unforgivable
youth.
in another turn, Rotation. I am Demeter
without Kore.
Furious.
Tantrumed.

I gave green
and harvest.
Remember your abundance.

Please
my
daughter
is missing.

past tensed, Did you
celebrate my gift?
Did you answer my mysteries? Eleusis
remembers me, arrival.
I am coming.
Persephone.

I can still
be the poppy,
while my child breathes
above ground
before the earth splits a wide throat,
and the king comes courting, calling his wife to their chamber
(damn you hades)
Until Eleusis remembers
I am calling,
coming,
Persephone!

                                          Kore!
                                    !we are dancing!
                                     until the hours
                                              turn.
                                    it will be time to

sleep
my love.

No Mafioso: This Way Through the Looking Glass Seeing You Seeing Me Seeing You Seeing Me Seeing You from Crosshatched Angles in Imprinted Set Type

Pompeii on our breaths we sat
stationed for the next train. How to clasp
Vesuviun ends in our chest? Like perverted
art cast a volcanic divine paper mache in death
throes. We breathed.
Free of cindered ash and ready for decay
we murmured over settlement around
extinction when he
elderly barreled and brimmed with meat
approached.
A cassette in his fist, he grinned.
Americano, si?
On a nod he said his words clumped and reshaped he said
my bambini love Americano, si?
He pushed the tape at us. We leaned
away and together. He said
Music, si. Americano. My babies love American.
Come with me, yes?
Alarm kindled away and together we leaned. He
raised his arms his two hands open at our direction. He said
No Mafioso no Mafioso no Mafioso.
Come with me, yes?
His head shaking our unspoken no.
Our heads shaking our unspoken no, until on that platform
Dani and me and that elderly not Mafioso man stood
caught all shaking together
a static interpretive La Tarantella chasing
away boogiemen and incubi premonitions. We
hung in awkward moments until his body
lopsided in regret backed away
his palms toward the ground tapped an
appeasing measure as he pivoted
to the stairs walking us watching

and breathing him leaving.
Dani elbow exclamation into my hip. She said
—we should have gone with him.—
—Are you crazy—
I said.
She said.
—It might have been fun—
—And he might have been a serial killer—
—you're being dramatic—
—he said no Mafioso like some sort of weird mantra
        What the hell was that?
        Why would he even say that?
        Why would he even think that we
        would even guess that he
        was even Mafia? Like just because
        we're in Italy, we think we're in the Godfather?—
Dani grinned said.
—maybe he was trying not to scare us?—
—So not successful! I bet we wake up with
equine body parts in our beds tomorrow...—
Shifting prickled in these slanted visions, we laughed
all our assumptive formulas between us. Let them sink
and ebb to the girded earth rest and macerate before the next othered
encounter.

Translation XLII

In here, somewhere, between rib spaces, intercostal webs stretched over these lungs filled and emptied. look left and find time stopped. Nothing happens here, we are safe in our flesh webbed cave. Find him harmless in this anxious womb nothing happens here. No slivered skins
No abraded elbows or knees
No twisted ligaments
No scarred tendons
No fractures
No
hiccupped breaths after tremor sobs.
Find him safe in my anxious womb, not weeping. Not
one thing happens. Inoculated numb, we are padded. No risk
No first times
No last times
No middles
No
hiccupped sobs after laughter.
Find him silent, or
rupture this trunk, splinter the frame jagged this caesarean wound, Yes!
He breathes messy asymmetrical gasps. He is scar wrapped. He is beautiful.

Translation XLIX

This first memory of: Do not look at the direct sun: Look to the side, above, or under, or squint, and blurry the view. Bleed this sun across the sky or you may go blind in her sight, they said, and I have passed this along, said onto my son. Don't look. I've led him away from stargazing, said, Don't look, She is too bright. She will not blink. Think twice about the scorched earth, the bitter evaporated salt, our caked skin. She is not forgiving. He still asks about the corona, its temperature: Is it as hot as the splitting sky, atoms cracked into blinding light? Imagine ruptured atoms and Ask: What does nuclear fusion look like without a man's slight hand or mathematical formulas branched out as chalkboard trees? How did we imagine this? Did someone see it first? Was someone god, lower or upper case important without religion, institutional followers, or bother-ers? Let's make holes in this dark matter, she said with her fingertip on fire hydrogen built into helium, make us fusion, make us combustible. How long did time take for the first hole to lose control, explode into a singularity? Did it guess we would theorize billions of years in the future about its existence, place lines and curves in an explanation-al order? Here, here is our portrait of a thing we cannot see. Is this comforting? When we look into light are we seeing the beginning of time, but wait, if we look closer still this gravity well, we are blind to everything but a radiating disk of stretched flight, so we hypothesize the unseen. Observe the bends in time, curves in light, guess at the center mass; this mess of out stretched arms swirling, let's draw symbols. Express the heart we can never look at directly or we look but do not see. We cannot find a thing, or we find it unobservable sitting just a little outside of our line of sight. Do we still believe? For all previously unseen things, we analyze the behavior of friendly objects, the motion of mates, the environmental dance: How this star moves binary, how this elliptical orbit shifts with a twin, swings a little wider with each twist or turn or pass; or how do we describe celestial mechanics; where Einstein becomes an alchemist and quantum equations become spells, and then wonders in all this explanation where is there room for wonder? Is it better to know, hypothesize, or guess than just let it sit? Do we want to know what makes the Milky Way twirl, and is there life after death? My son asks, Is Daddy waiting for me? Do you think he sees me? Does he know how old I'll be when I die? I ask, will my son remember how much he is loved, when I am gone? I know the world will spin in the same direction; the magnetic poles will shift by fractions; the continents will make contact again, but move a little closer in now, will my son have his own children? Will he love them as fragments, or universal, integral to a bigger picture? Will he believe there is no such thing as small beings, just degrees of separation necessary for existing? Will he come to my conclusion: I cannot love you all the same without disintegrating in a flame of loving you too much for this body to hold. I am too close to too full already, but I've seen you camera caught in magazines and TV screens. You were in front of your leveled house. You were huddled bunched body over your dead children. You were a blank stare standing at the grave of your machete-massacred family, and I flinched, and then looked away. I have been in this picture. Camera caught with my son, we were hand in hand with grief, then hypothetically diagnosed with PTSD. Sometimes our lives are equated to bear like E=MC2. We become relative instead of related. How do I care when you are a stranger? So you are relative to how well I know you, or someone who loves you. If I know your first name, see you every day, then somehow your everyday detail transforms to significance, rather than any other small moment in some other life I might pretend to believe, but bottom line I am blind when I wish I could see through this dark matter to the sun, who blisters my son with her kiss. If you stand back far enough she says, I look just like Andromeda's nebula mists.

Cultural Experience: As in Memories Based on Colluded Definitions Classifications and Characterizations, Not Real Time Tours of Battlefield Historical Sites and Beautiful Bodies

A week in
we figured we were game
> *she says as in predator hunting Game*
> *prey for food and*
> *sport usually land based often*
> *mammalian and rarely*
> *domesticated not chess nor sorry*
> *nor monopoly nor texas hold `em nor*
> *football nor air hockey nor halo nor you*
> *got game as in skilled or spunky nor*
> *A game as in the best game playing*
> *in the game.*

One of us was approached
in the Tesco. His bearing cautious, at first, he
asked her where she was
from, but when he heard her
accent, his net became tangible. He said
I've always heard Americans are easy
> *she says as in referring to promiscuous behavior*
> *maybe even lasciviousness possibly*
> *multi-partnered and never*
> *too picky, but definitely not a computer script nor*
> *a song nor a film nor a Louisiana city nor*
> *a LA rapper who founded NWA changed*
> *the face of hip hop, fought and then made*
> *up with Dr. Dre, and then died of complications*
> *due to an AIDS related illness at the age of*
> *31.*

She said well
I guess you're going to keep on just
hearing about that, aren't you.

A month in
we were a little pissed
> *she says as in angry or infuriated or filled with*
> *wrath not drunk nor sozzled nor inebriated*
> *nor sloshed nor tipsy nor wankered nor*
> *three sheets to the wind.*

a little tired of getting solicited
we had ovaries and a blue passport
this was not the education we sought in
antique halls walking aged timbers tracing their
history on rub worn balustrades and railings.

Three months in
with so much to choose from flirting
choice fleshy morsels of good sturdy old world stock
we said fuck it
> *she says as in never mind or whatever or forget it or*
> *I give up or I give in or I don't care or whatevas*
> *or if you can't beat 'em join 'em not fornicate with*
> *it nor have sex with it nor make love to it nor*
> *screw it nor copulate with it nor free love with*
> *it nor sleep with it nor cohabitate with it nor*
> *fuck it.*

But it kind of was fuck it
> *as in we thought why not and*
> *called this our seminal cultural experience.*

Translation LVI

Full body amour
Enveloped chainmail and blood music, is this why
we hold the shell to our ear?
Try eidetic. Totally recall a back story. Hear the ocean as
your soundtrack. Do you remember when you were swimming
never hungry
never cold?

Do you covet amnesiac moments?
Rather remember the amniotic red cloud before your closed eyes?
Did you taste it?   let the color roll across your tongue and blossom
Did you hear music
in your fingers?   somatic sounds sort out to epithelia symphonies
Did you write your self a book?   cover to cover without auto
Did you fight   dig anchors into soft walls—
        when the amour was chinked, when the maille was unraveling,
                when you were unsure she wanted you to stay.

Killer Conscience

In standing room only
between Rome and Naples
at the end of questing fingers and assaulting limbs
it became easy to model victim.
We learned this posture so young
between the legs of Barbie
and Charlie's Angels rubbing thumbs
on bodies devoid of familiar features. These girls
were never my sisters, but
they taught me the ideal man
came with a soundtrack. That
he was blond
and plastic with a mouth guard for teeth
and hips that moved in only two directions.
That he had some assembly required and
was best heard through a speaker phone or
a sweet sexless man translator. This space
left no room for risk for hormones for contradictions
for unexpected gifts for battle for ball wrecking
joy standing between Rome and Naples
cornered by foreign inhibition and reckless adolescence found me
interpreting myself as quarry in knee jerking
wanting to butt the stump heel of my palm against their
plastic jaws. Hoped I'd see their skulls snap back to spines.
Mimic an avian death arch of contracting muscles. But
standing between Rome and Naples we only swayed to the metal track.
Our eyes swept the floor; gaze never swinging above
knees believing *if we don't see them they*
won't hurt us, and in our unresponsive silence
their curling fingers retracted. They did not push.
So standing years later as
after thoughts and epilogues interrupt this status; discover a slow
footnote to caution to rejected overtures as we blurred
through their sovereignty. See I was just
a visitor

with my half shunned encumbered nationhood clutched in pockets
as a concealed weapon. Always under breath
never said yes, Americans are easy, but if
you hurt us
we
will kill you.

East *zero point nihil*

still
not
fr
ee

island

only myth   getaway
potatoes   small
religion   crimped
war | only pink
foreign   sun
exotica   dawn

setting

loves

pressed fodder
through kings'
giant canons.
they
swung
sun king   big guns
and silk   strategic
geopolitical
they   sub
never   mission
bonjour
drank   gutter tag
achewed
cream.

Siegfried
(poor lad)
always stretch-
ing for the
out of
reach brass
always
swatted
down.
impudent
Child.

These buggers. They crossed
oceans(plural!) to be in me.
maybe small, yet
so determined, They nicked
me in generations. Embedded
in brown. *Did she choose? Fuck.*
Swabbed floors and counters, but
imagine them equal and laugh.
Gentle conquerors...a punch lined.

zero is a number is a naught

59

can I have a desert can I have a desert

PACIFIC COORDINATES

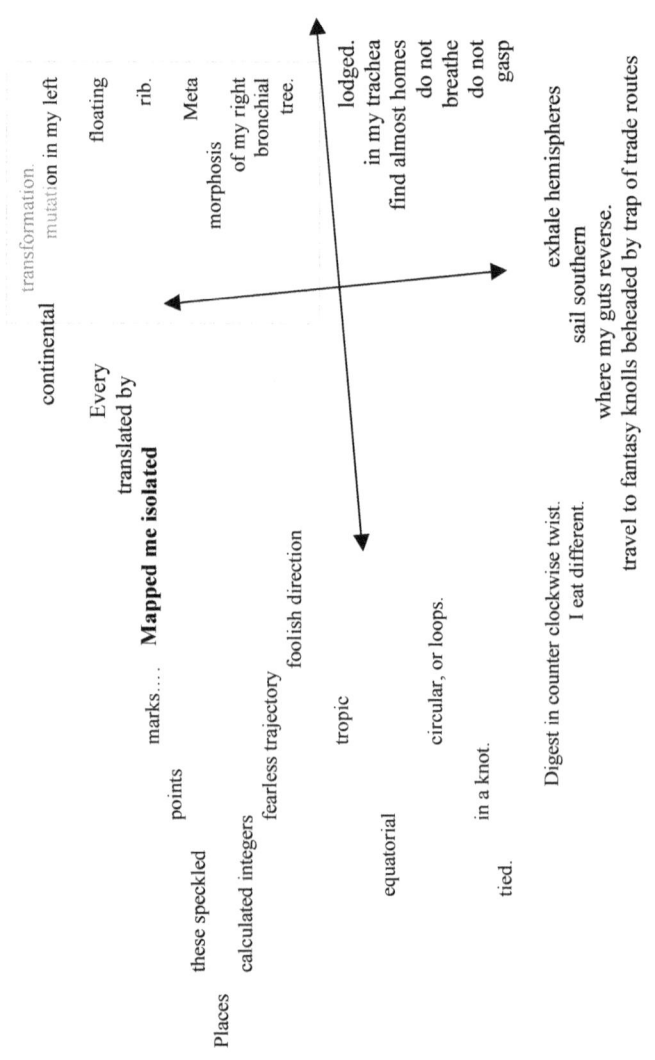

transformation
mutation in my left

floating

rib.

continental

Meta
morphosis
of my right
bronchial
tree.

lodged.
in my trachea
find almost homes
do not
breathe
do not
gasp

Every
translated by

Mapped me isolated

exhale hemispheres
sail southern
where my guts reverse.
travel to fantasy knolls beheaded by trap of trade routes

marks....

foolish direction

fearless trajectory

points

these speckled

Places

calculated integers

tropic

equatorial

circular, or loops.

in a knot.

tied.

Digest in counter clockwise twist.
I eat different.

Yes

Some days I say no
never yes and hate
the n   the o
between my tongue and teeth
my cavity closing to a kiss.

Can I have dessert   No?
Can I stay up late   No?
Can I have so/so come over to play   No?
Can I watch south park   No?
Can I play dsi   No?
Can I have this   No?
Can I throw that   No?
Can I ask   No?
        A question   No.

Translation LXIII

Wake up alarm snooze ten maybe twenty minutes out of bed race to the bathroom whose turn is it to walk the dog. Pour coffee, thank the celestial bodies, and drink. Start the packed lunch in plastic containers so we're not too disposable, has he fed the cat yet? Is he dressed? She is taking a slow breath. The car is leaking oil again. Dog's in the backseat howling at a passing walker they're passing.

They go in separate pieces in his thoughts he has games and strategy and plots, while she has worry and forget in her head wondering what will be remembered and what will be left undone waiting for the next to do later. The list never gets shorter. The emails, the phone calls, the texts, the letters sprawled and spiraled into spins as if a black hole is at the center of this.

Get in the car and don't forget to check the gas gauge. She can't be late, because they charge by the second. Open the door. He's had a good day. He shows her sketches. He sings songs with his full throat open wide. He asks what does she think, does she like it even a bit. That's an easy answer she says

                                                                    Yes.

Translation LXX

as unoriginal as breathing as burnt as a sonnet as played as twenty
centuries as worn as belief as under this sun as arbitrary as picking
random letters from alphabet soup
spelling kdjfkjklwoeoeojcikeaajo, because this
is what these fingers choose like speaking in Greek.

translate:sun:god:goddess:
sol:sole:shemesh:jua:aurinko:surya:soleil:taiyou:
haul:son:zon:ilanga:sonne:araw: ἥλιος

Midnight Mass

Because we stayed when
they said we could leave when
Christmas Eve was a reminder we
were so far from home and gifts were
tickets and minutes of the day in yesterday's
clothes spoiled rotten.

Because we stayed they asked
they said it's small, but there will be enough
food. Yes, you will be welcome because you did
not leave. You should not be without family on the eve
before Christmas.

It was small. A room. A family table.
Benches and bowls of food. Yes, please
help yourself, as we nod through language
after language barrier. At 1am after mass we
pulled tables and chairs, butted them to the walls,
and danced until thighs shook with all that worship.

Welcome

Spotting red across midnight
Losing in 12 weeks when embryo
swimming just fetal almost
breathing
without oxygen.
his face a picture.
eyes with lids.
fingers in a fist.
lanugo skullcap

almost gone almost gone almost a lost letter almost static almost
noise....but

                         cyclical sound *p r e s s s u r e* image

him still there in my fundal cushion
captured
growing
                this relief.

Rest Here

This anabolic shape
brings suspension.
He fights these
inanimate limbs he
must get every
waking turbulent limbic
imprint before eye
movements rapid fire
his systems. It is
time for bed, my
sweetness.

Translation LXXVII

These are just words.
So easy to tear letter from
letter to torn symbols and speech
becomes imagined. Let's write a
new language in biology in sub-atomic
in program in particles in stellar structures where
he is math; she is physics;
we become shapes and brush strokes.
we become a character
letter.
Mid-life only forty
or four billion years more
before rest, so she
tries not to sleep. He agrees
at five minutes after midnight
he'd rather keep reading beneath
a night light or flashlight. Mommy
he says, can't you read us
in these margins.

Embraced by Buddha
You departed to a Western Shore
Beloved image vanished…
how sad we are!
Embraced by Buddha
You went to Compassionate Land
By example teaching the way to salvation…
how grateful we are!
Embrace Buddha
Depart to Precious Abode
Become on with holy Buddha
how sacred you are!

When You Are Tired

Translate who
we are behind big questions where
according to Adams
every answer under the sun is
always 42. Let's talk
science where
life is probability paradox or equation where
we can guess if we happened before or
if we could happen again in investigating
$N=R^* \times f_p \times n_e \times f_e \times f_i \times f_c \times L$ *as proposed by Drake*
or
$Ff^2(MgE) - C^1Ri^1 \times M = L/So$ *as interpreted by Roddenberry*
or
talk to Fermi and add in the variables
or
ask are we alone where
how many knowns are known where
we don't know the primordial planets scattered
passed the speed of flight estranged as second
cousins removed forty-two times. Improbable Black Swan
Events: ....*rara avis in terris nigroque simillima cygno*....where
all swan feathers must be white where
being and event collide where
a singular moment can re-direct our perception of time.

This is where I am at the end of a universe
middle aged under a middle aged sun where
20 years from today
seems too close
too quick to clasp
unknown happens
unpredicted undirected indescribable
in inaccessible distance.
Because if I go here:
to general relativity to the end
of the galaxy and back to

where I translate him to un petit prince
sitting   cross-legged   on   Cyngus   X-1's   wrist
in   Orion's   arm
of   a   spinning   spiral   spun
around at least one speculation becoming our singularity
forming   a   cupped   fist   skin
containing   the   mass   of   a   billion   suns
becoming static
becoming statistic becoming
one million to one and
I don't have to go here:
to seconds to minutes to
hours to days
to the day after today
where he becomes another galaxy

will he still love dogs
will he watch Scooby Doo
will he still struggle with chopsticks
will he love french fries and chocolate
will he still collect everything
imaginable
will he speak in another language?

today the universe is not ending.
In an elliptical whirl
on this blue green
world, he is growing up
I am holding my hands
folded   trying not to
grasp too tight
But
here
he is in the next room sleeping
my safe self cradled
in his awkward limbs. Tell him it's time
to go to sleep, sometimes

                                        he will go/or
        protest in brief when today this universe is not ending
                                            I am
                                            still
                                          Mommy
                                 when no one else is
                                        listening.

3y3 1()\/3 j()Y3W _7ayeiX()8

Me ke aloha nui ia oukou pakahi a pau...

Another book could be written thanking people who have nurtured me and supported the time and space I give to poetry, but I will pay homage to my slam poetry connections and attempt to flavor my remarks with a spice of brevity.

Much of this collection would not exist without the graduate classes and poetry workshops at the University of Hawai'i at Mānoa. I offer my thanks to those creative rooms and voices and to everyone who works in the English Department at University of Hawai'i at Mānoa. Thank you to Tinfish Press and Susan Schultz.

Enormous amounts of gratitude are given to all of Pacific Tongues. You give me breath. I give a special thanks to Rajiv Mohabir, who has gone above and beyond the call as a mentor, cheerleader, and dear friend. His encouragement and support breathes in every page of this book. In equal measure, I thank Craig Santos Perez, as mentor and friend; he always helps me continue believing in the work and the importance of our Pacific community. Thank you to Jonathan Kay Kamakawiwo'ole Osorio, Laura Lyons, Craig Howes, Cynthia Franklin, and Cristina Bacchilega for their continued and amazing support through a rather long and windy journey.

Thank you to Brenda Shaughnessy for her voice in the world and her kind and ever-generous encouragement.

Hugs, kisses, and love to Jamaica Heolimeleikalani Osorio, Donovan Kūhiō Colleps, No'u Revilla, Kim Compoc, Serena Simmons, Aiko Yamashiro, Harrison Ines, Travis Kaulula'au Thompson, Melvin Won Pat-Borja, Jason Mateo, Sterling Higa, Will Giles, and Anjoli Roy. For David Keali'i Mackenzie and Bryan Kamaoli Kuwada, for their endless willingness to listen and to read and to open their generous hearts, no laua kuu mahalo nui a me ke aloha nui pu. I give love and thanks to Joy Enomoto for all her gorgeous art, our friendship, and for our sustaining artistic collaborations.

Grace Taylor has been endlessly sustaining and full of heart. Mahalo nui loa, Sis. Thank you to Jocelyn Ng, with her vision, abundant energy, and eloquent commitment, she makes the future possible, and I am so looking forward to seeing more of her artistry out in the world.

To Hawaiʻi, to the ʻāina, to the diasporic settler, and indigenous communities that offer safe haven and home, salamat po, dòjeh, thank you, arigatou, mahalo nui loa.

For my parents, I find my words inadequate. My mother and father have been endlessly fortifying with their patience and love. Thank you and I love you is not enough.

Finally, thank you to Jakob, my son, who sat patiently through countless poetry readings and who inspired much of this book with his lovely astonishing soul.

W inner of the 2014 Ian MacMillan contest for poetry, **Lyz Soto** is a performance poet and co-founder of Pacific Tongues. She is a long time mentor and coach with its award winning youth poetry program, Youth Speaks Hawaiʻi, which won the Brave New Voices International Poetry competition in 2008 and 2009, and continues to push the boundaries in spoken arts performance. She has performed in Hawaiʻi, Aotearoa, Papua New Guinea and the continental United States, and her poetry has been read before the president of Vanuatu. In addition to her performances, she has been published in *Hawaii Review, blackmail press 36 - Banninur: A Basket of Food, The Hawaiʻi Independent, Ke Kaʻupu Hehi ʻAle, Na Hua Ea,* and *Damfino.* Her chapbook *Eulogies* was published in 2010 by TinFish Press. Lyz is working on completing a PhD in English at University of Hawaiʻi at Mānoa, where she teaches composition, spoken arts, Pacific literature, and creative writing. In December 2016, *Her Bodies of Stories,* her first full length spoken arts theater show premiered at the Doris Duke Theater in Honolulu, Hawaiʻi.

www.ingramcontent.com/pod-product-compliance
Lightning Source LLC
Chambersburg PA
CBHW021155090426
42740CB00008B/1100